EXTREME SPORTS
No Limits!

Extreme Skiing

Kelley MacAulay & Bobbie Kalman

Crabtree Publishing Company

www.crabtreebooks.com

Created by Bobbie Kalman

Dedicated by Katherine Kantor
Mojim kochanym rodzicom chrzesnym, wujkowi Kazikowi i cioci Jadzi Sobolewskim

Editor-in-Chief
Bobbie Kalman

Writing team
Kelley MacAulay
Bobbie Kalman

Substantive editor
Kathryn Smithyman

Editors
Molly Aloian
Robin Johnson
Rebecca Sjonger

Design
Katherine Kantor

Production coordinator
Heather Fitzpatrick

Photo research
Crystal Foxton

Consultant
Peter Judge, CEO, Canadian Freestyle Ski Association

Illustrations
Katherine Kantor: pages 11, 15
Robert MacGregor: page 9
Bonna Rouse: page 10

Photographs
Icon SMI: Tony Donaldson: pages 18, 21; DPPI: page 20;
    Mike Ridewood: pages 12, 13, 29; Sport the library: pages 22, 28
Special Collections Dept., J. Willard Marriott Library,
    University of Utah: pages 6, 7
Manna Photography: © George & Judy Manna: page 24;
    © Judy Manna: page 19
Eric Schramm: page 23
Shazamm: page 14
© Copyright 2005 Paul Thomas (MotionImaging.co.uk): pages 16-17
Olympic Parks of Utah: page 25
Other images by Adobe Image Library, Digital Vision, and Photodisc

Crabtree Publishing Company

www.crabtreebooks.com   1-800-387-7650

Cataloging-in-Publication Data
MacAulay, Kelley.
  Extreme skiing / Kelley MacAulay & Bobbie Kalman.
    p. cm. -- (Extreme sports no limits!)
  Includes index.
  ISBN-13: 978-0-7787-1682-2 (rlb)
  ISBN-10: 0-7787-1682-1 (rlb)
  ISBN-13: 978-0-7787-1728-7 (pbk)
  ISBN-10: 0-7787-1728-3 (pbk)
  1. Freestyle skiing--Juvenile literature. 2. Extreme sports--Juvenile literature.
I. Kalman, Bobbie. II. Title. III. Series.
  GV854.9.F74M33 2006
  797.93'7--dc22
                                                    2005035789
                                                    LC

**Published in
the United States**

PMB16A
350 Fifth Ave.
Suite 3308
New York, NY
10118

**Published
in Canada**

616 Welland Ave.
St. Catharines, Ontario
Canada
L2M 5V6

**Published in the
United Kingdom**

White Cross Mills
High Town, Lancaster
LA1 4XS
United Kingdom

**Published
in Australia**

386 Mt. Alexander Rd.
Ascot Vale (Melbourne)
VIC 3032

CONTENTS

EXTREME SKIING

Extreme skiing, or freestyle skiing, is a thrilling **extreme sport** that is popular around the world. Extreme sports are challenging events that encourage athletes to push themselves to the limits of their abilities. Extreme skiers strive to be creative by trying tricks that have never been done before. The top freestyle skiers make a living by taking part in freestyle skiing competitions. They train year round to learn skills and to develop daring new tricks that combine skiing with challenging **acrobatics**.

TEAM PLAYERS

Many top skiers belong to teams, which are **sponsored** by companies that design and make skis and gear. Freestyle skiing is an **individual sport**, however. In an individual sport, the athletes do not compete as part of a team.

*To many freestyle skiers, freestyle is not just a sport—it is a **culture**. A culture is a set of values that a group of people share. Freestyle skiing culture includes its own **lingo**, or language, a relaxed clothing style, and a good sense of fun!*

SKIING STYLES

There are three main styles of freestyle skiing: **freeride**, **moguls**, and **aerials**. Freeride skiers continually develop tricks and take part in different competitions. Mogul skiers ski down steep slopes that are covered with mounds of snow called moguls. Athletes taking part in aerial competitions launch themselves off huge snow-covered **ramps**, or jumps, and perform tricks such as **flips** and **spins** in the air!

FREE AT LAST

Some freestyle skiers also enjoy **freeskiing**. Freeskiers seek out the **back country**, where few other skiers dare to go. Freeskiers hike up mountains so they can ski down rough **terrain** and jump off cliffs, as shown right.

EXTREME DANGER!

As you read this book, keep in mind that top freestyle skiers train for years to master their sport. Only trained skiers should attempt freestyle skiing.

FREESTYLE: THE BEGINNING

People have been skiing in Europe for thousands of years. In the past, skiing was simply a way for people to get around in winter. It wasn't until the mid 1800s that people in Europe began skiing for fun. Around the same time, Norwegian and Swedish **immigrants** introduced skiing to people in the United States.

TAKING IT TO THE EXTREME

In the 1950s, an American named Stein Eriksen, who is known as the "father of freestyle skiing," began drawing huge crowds at Sunday afternoon ski shows in Sun Valley, Idaho. Eriksen performed front and back flips on skis, which people had never seen before. By the 1960s, Eriksen had inspired other skiers, who tried new tricks and organized freestyle skiing competitions. These competitions were soon attracting spectators from around the world.

GAINING POPULARITY

At first, skiing was not popular in America, but the invention of the **rope tow** in the 1940s changed skiing forever. The rope tow was a device that pulled skiers to the top of mountains. Before the rope tow was invented, skiers had to trudge up steep, snowy mountainsides. The rope tow saved people time and allowed them to make several **runs**, or trips down mountains, each day.

This picture shows a crowd of skiers waiting to use a rope tow in 1943.

BREAKING THE RULES

In 1979, freestyle skiing was recognized as an official sport by the Fédération Internationale de Ski (FIS). The FIS soon helped form rules for freestyle skiing competitions. For example, mogul skiers were no longer allowed to perform tricks upside down. Some skiers felt that the rules limited their creativity. In spite of the rules, many skiers continued performing spectacular new tricks at competitions. The creation of the **X Games** in 1995 helped spark an extreme sports boom, which pushed sports such as freestyle skiing into the spotlight. Today, athletes are creating even more daring moves, earning freestyle skiing its reputation as one of the most exciting extreme sports.

The efforts of freestyle skiers in the 1970s and 1980s helped pave the way for freestyle skiing to become an exciting extreme sport. One of these skiers was Bob Theobald, who is shown above.

TIMELINE

*1965: An Austrian gymnast named Hermann Goellner achieves the first **double flip** on skis.*
1966: The first organized freestyle skiing event takes place in Waterville Valley, New Hampshire.
1969: The first film about freestyle skiing, The Moebius Flip, *is released in the United States.*
1974: Amateur freestyle skiing takes shape in Canada, when John Johnston creates the Canadian Freestyle Skiers Association.
1976: The first Nationals competition is held in Canada.

1978: The first World Cup competition is held.
1981: The first FIS-organized World Cup competition is held.
1986: The first FIS Freestyle World Championships are held.
1992: Moguls makes its first appearance as a medal event in the Winter Olympics.
1994: Aerials makes its first appearance as a medal event in the Winter Olympics.
*2002: **Superpipe** and **slopestyle** events are added to the Winter X Games.*

SKI ANATOMY

The first skis were heavy wooden boards that did not slide easily over snow. All that has changed, however! Today's skis are made of smooth, durable, and **flexible** materials that can take a beating.

THE SKIS

All skis are made up of the same basic parts. The **core**, or center, of a ski is made of wood or foam. The core is wrapped in **fiberglass**, which is a strong but lightweight material. The core is covered on top and on both sides by a one-piece **cap**, which is also usually made of fiberglass. The cap is covered by a **top skin**, or a protective sheeting that often has **graphics** on it. The **base**, or bottom of the ski, is made of strong, slippery plastic. Polished strips of metal along the sides of a ski help it cut into snow.

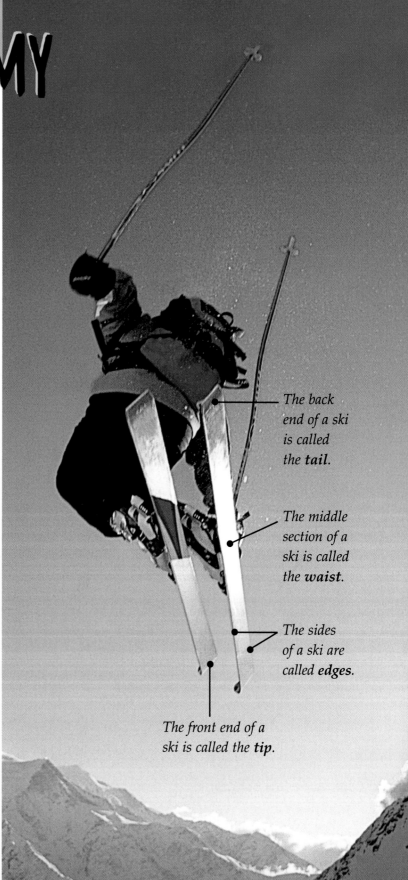

The back end of a ski is called the **tail**.

The middle section of a ski is called the **waist**.

The sides of a ski are called **edges**.

The front end of a ski is called the **tip**.

So Many Styles

Each style of freestyle skiing requires a different type of ski. Each type of ski is a different width and length. Most also have different **sidecuts** and flexibility. Sidecut is the inward curve on the side of a ski. Skis with deep sidecuts are best for making wide turns. Skis with shallow sidecuts are used for making sharp turns. The different skis used in freestyle skiing are shown below.

*Freeride skiers use **twin-tip skis**. Twin-tip skis curve upward at both ends, allowing skiers to perform more tricks and to ride **fakie**, or backward. Freeride skis also have deep sidecuts.*

Mogul skis are long and flexible. Their shape allows the skis to smash down on moguls without snapping. Mogul skis have soft tips, which absorb the impact of the moguls, giving skiers greater stability. The skis also have shallow sidecuts, since the skiers do not make wide turns.

Aerial skis are usually lightweight and shorter than the skier who is using them. Shorter skis allow aerial skiers to control their movements in the air better than longer skis do.

*Freeskiers use **fat skis**, or extra-wide skis. These skis are also often thicker than other types of skis. Wide, thick skis are able to absorb the impact of hard landings.*

GET IN GEAR

Extreme skiing is a lot of fun, but skiers need to suit up in the right gear before they hit the slopes. Using the proper gear and wearing protective clothing helps keep skiers safe while they enjoy their sport.

BALANCING ACT

Skiers use poles for some styles of freestyle skiing. Mogul skiers make sharp, fast turns, and they use their poles to help them turn at the right moment. Skiers also use poles to help them land after performing in the **halfpipe**, in moguls, or in freeskiing. Halfpipes are U-shaped ditches that are designed to launch skiers into the air. Aerial skiers do not use poles.

BOOT IT

Ski boots have tough plastic **shells**, or outer coverings, that protect a skier's feet. They also have thick inner linings that cushion a skier's feet and keep them warm and dry. Ski boots are attached to skis by metal or plastic clips called **bindings**. Although all ski boots are tough, some are more flexible than others. Mogul skiers usually choose stiffer boots, whereas aerial skiers wear softer boots that allow their ankles to be straight during takeoffs. Freeride skiers also prefer flexible boots, which allow the skiers to move freely while performing tricks.

HEADGEAR

Freestyle skiers travel at high speeds and often find themselves upside down as they perform tricks! They wear helmets to protect their heads during **wipeouts**, or crashes. Helmets have hard outer shells made of plastic and insides that are made of foam. These materials are strong and lightweight. To keep warm, most skiers wear thick winter hats beneath their helmets.

WINTER WEAR

Freestyle skiers must wear several layers of clothing to protect their skin from cold winter weather. Layers of clothing also add padding that helps cushion falls. The first layer usually consists of **thermal** underwear and socks, a fleece sweater, and comfortable pants. These clothes trap a skier's body heat, which helps keep him or her warm and dry. This layer of clothes is covered by a waterproof ski jacket and snow pants. If the day warms up, the skier can always remove a layer of clothing.

GOGGLES

Skiers wear **goggles** to protect their eyes from the wind and from small pieces of flying ice and snow. Goggles also block harmful **ultraviolet rays** and can prevent a skier from getting **snow blindness**.

goggles

helmet

*Freeskiers and many freeride skiers wear hard plastic elbow pads and knee pads. The pads help reduce the risk of injuries caused by contact with hard snow, ice, and **obstacles**, or objects in the way.*

FREERIDE

Like many other extreme sports, freeride skiing was inspired by the thrilling stunts developed by extreme skateboarders in the early 1970s. Freeride skiing is also known as **new school**. This style of skiing encourages skiers to be creative as they adapt old tricks and try new tricks that test the limits of their courage. Top freeride skiers perform complex tricks that combine some of the basic moves described on these pages.

SLIDES

Many skiers perform **slide** tricks in **terrain parks**. To perform slides, skiers glide their skis across obstacles such as **boxes** or metal rails. Boxes are raised platforms. Skiers require great balance if they are to slide to the end of the rails!

GRABS

Skiers often combine **grabs**, shown above, with other tricks to make their performances more impressive to judges. To perform grab tricks, skiers bend their bodies and take hold of parts of their skis. A popular grab is the **mute grab**. To perform a mute grab, a skier bends down and takes hold of the tip of his or her ski while in midair.

SPINS AND TWISTS

Spin tricks are also called **twists**. To perform spin tricks, skiers **rotate**, or turn around, in the air before landing. Spins are named for the number of times a skier rotates in the air. A half rotation is called a **180** because the skier makes a half turn of 180° in the air. A full rotation is called a **360** because the skier rotates full circle, or 360°. Top skiers are very creative and learn to take off and land backward or forward while performing multiple spins, such as the **540** (one-and-a-half turns,) the **720** (two turns,) or the **1080** (three turns).

FLIPS

To perform a flip trick, a skier turns head over heels while in midair. Flip tricks are difficult moves that take years of training to master. The skier shown right is performing a flip during a competition.

IN THE PARK

Many ski resorts now have terrain parks, where freeride skiers can invent and practice tricks on obstacles without damaging public property! Terrain parks for skiers and snowboarders are modeled after **skateparks**. Skateparks are concrete terrain parks where skateboarders create their moves. Terrain parks are full of different obstacles. Each obstacle provides skiers with new challenges and opportunities. Skiing on obstacles allows skiers to test their instincts and to develop skills such as balance and coordination.

This freeride skier is riding a rail at a terrain park.

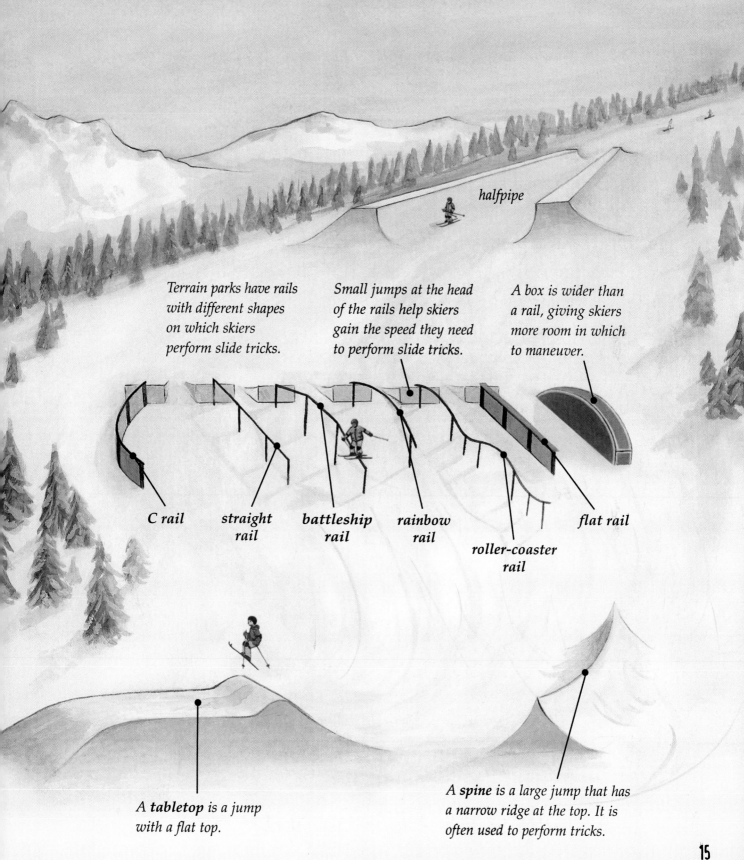

halfpipe

Terrain parks have rails with different shapes on which skiers perform slide tricks.

Small jumps at the head of the rails help skiers gain the speed they need to perform slide tricks.

A box is wider than a rail, giving skiers more room in which to maneuver.

C rail

straight rail

battleship rail

rainbow rail

roller-coaster rail

flat rail

A **tabletop** is a jump with a flat top.

A **spine** is a large jump that has a narrow ridge at the top. It is often used to perform tricks.

15

IN THE PIPE

In order to perform flip, spin, and grab tricks, freeride skiers need to **get air**, or fly up into the air. The halfpipe provides skiers with the ideal terrain for getting air and pulling off advanced moves. The two sloping sides of the halfpipe are called **transitions**. To ski in the halfpipe, a skier stands at the **lip**, or top edge of a transition, and then slides down the transition. Next, the skier slides up the facing transition and flies into the air! The skier must have great coordination to perform a trick and get back into position before landing on the transition once again.

SUPER SIZE IT!

Skiers who want the ultimate halfpipe experience ride the superpipe! The superpipe is a super-sized halfpipe that is popular in competitions. Halfpipe transitions can be up to 15 feet (4.6 m) high, but superpipe transitions are often 18 feet (5.5 m) high! In competitions, skiers perform in the pipe individually. Skiers have only a few minutes to impress the judges, so they pull off as many gutsy tricks as possible to make an impression.

SKIER X

Skier X is a daring freeride competition that includes elements of **motocross**, a motorcycle sport in which a group of riders races on an outdoor course. In skier X competitions, four to six skiers compete against one another **simultaneously**, or at the same time. The skiers race down a steep course that is covered with a variety of challenges such as jumps, tabletops, and **banked**, or angled, turns.

The obstacles and the extreme speed test a skier's ability to **strategize**, or plan, his or her next move quickly. Skier X is a timed event, so there are no judges at the competitions. The fastest skier in each round moves on to the final round. The fastest skier in the final round is declared the winner. There are so many obstacles on the course, however, that skiers often **collide** before crossing the finish line!

THE ULTIMATE CHALLENGE

Ultracross is the only freestyle skiing event in which the athletes compete in teams. It is a new event that pairs the top sixteen skiers from a skier X competition with the top sixteen snowboarders from a **boardercross competition**. Boardercross competitions are similar to skier X competitions, but instead of riding skis, the athletes ride snowboards. For ultracross, each skier is randomly paired up with a snowboarder. The snowboarders race against one another first. As soon as a snowboarder crosses the finish line, his or her skier X teammate bursts out of the starting gate and races to the finish line! The team that has the fastest combined time wins the competition.

Ultracross competitions take place on skier X courses.

SLOPESTYLE

Slopestyle is a freeride skiing competition that was added to the Winter X Games in 2002. In slopestyle competitions, skiers compete individually on a course filled with obstacles such as rails, boxes, and jumps, which are usually found in terrain parks. Skiers move through the course and use the obstacles to perform as many new tricks as they can. The areas between the obstacles are flat. Flat runs allow skiers to regain their speed between tricks. Slopestyle competitions showcase the latest tricks invented by skiers.

TABLETOP

Tabletop competitions are freeride events that are also known as **big air**. In tabletop, competitors fly off ramps and then perform tricks in the air. Skiers taking part in tabletop competitions are even allowed to take off from the ramp and land backward! Most skiers perform **off-axis** flips and spins. In off-axis tricks, a skier's body is level with the ground during the trick.

Competitors are judged on how much air they get off the ramp, on their landings, and on how much they can **tweak out a trick**! To tweak out a trick is to perform the trick in the most extreme way possible. For example, a skier may tweak out a trick by bending his or her body into an unusual position, as shown in the picture above.

21

MOGUL MANIA

Mogul competitors wear knee pads that are not the same color as the color of their ski pants, so the judges will notice their exact movements.

In moguls, skiers speed down steep **mogul fields,** or hills covered with moguls. Mogul fields are between 660 to 900 feet (201 to 274 m) long. Mogul competitors must think ahead in order to maintain control as they absorb hard landings on the moguls and make turns at the same time. To make things even more challenging, each mogul field includes two sets of ramps that launch skiers into the air. While in the air, skiers perform tricks such as spins, flips, and **uprights.** Seven judges score the skiers on how well they control their turns, their tricks in the air, and their speed.

TRICKSTERS

In the past, mogul skiers were limited in the types of tricks they could perform at competitions. Today, many types of tricks are allowed. Skiers can perform off-axis moves, as well as single flips with up to two twists. Mogul skiers are even allowed to attempt 1080 spins!

DUAL MOGULS

Dual mogul competitions take place at FIS World Championships. During dual mogul events, skiers take on a mogul field two at a time. The challenge of racing head-to-head with other athletes brings out the aggressive nature of the skiers, as they struggle to beat one another's best times.

The intense competition encourages racers to increase their speed, but the fastest skier does not necessarily win the race. The rules for judging dual mogul events are the same as those used in moguls. Athletes must maintain control as they turn over the moguls and perform a variety of tricks in the air.

AIR TIME

Skiers taking part in aerial competitions are serious thrill seekers! In aerials, athletes ski off large, steep ramps called **kickers** and launch themselves up to 50 feet (15.2 m) in the air. Many athletes hit their ramps at speeds of up to 43 miles per hour (69.2 kph)! In the air, the athletes perform tricks such as somersaults with twists before landing back on the ground. The athletes perform two jumps each. Seven judges mark the athletes on their takeoffs, on the heights and lengths of their jumps, on their landings, and most importantly, on their precise form.

Aerial competitors hit kickers at very high speeds! The intense speed gives them the height they need to perform spectacular aerial tricks.

HEAD OVER HEELS?

There are two types of aerial competitions: upright and **inverted**. In upright aerials, an athlete's feet must not go over his or her head. In inverted aerials, skiers can perform tricks while upside down. Before skiers are allowed to perform tricks in competitions, they must prove their abilities by performing their tricks safely into a swimming pool, where water cushions their landings, as shown below.

BACKCOUNTRY BOUND

Skiers who want the ultimate adventure hike up backcountry mountains to experience freeskiing. The back country offers skiers two skiing surfaces: rough mountain terrain and light, untouched **powder**. Powder is soft, deep snow. Freeskiers race down steep, rocky mountainsides, jump off cliffs that are up to 40 feet (12.2 m) high, and land in powder! Powder provides skiers with soft landing spots.

NATURAL TERRAIN PARKS

Freeskiers in the back country use obstacles found in nature to perform many of the tricks freeride skiers perform in terrain parks. Rocks, fallen logs, and snowdrifts provide great opportunities for slide tricks and for catching some air! Freeskiers often seek out **bowls**. Bowls are giant open areas usually found on the back sides of mountains. Bowls have deep powder and steep-sloping sides, which the skiers use like halfpipe transitions.

BE SAFE

Backcountry skiing may sound like fun, but it can be very dangerous! Freeskiers are at risk of being caught in **avalanches**. Also, skiers who are injured while in the back country may be far from help. To be safe, freeskiers should never travel alone into the back country. They also need to carry a lot of equipment with them up the mountains. Every skier should have a compass, a watch, a shovel, and an **avalanche bleeper**. An avalanche bleeper is equipment that makes a loud noise so rescuers can find someone who has been buried in an avalanche. Skiers should also listen to weather reports before heading into the back country.

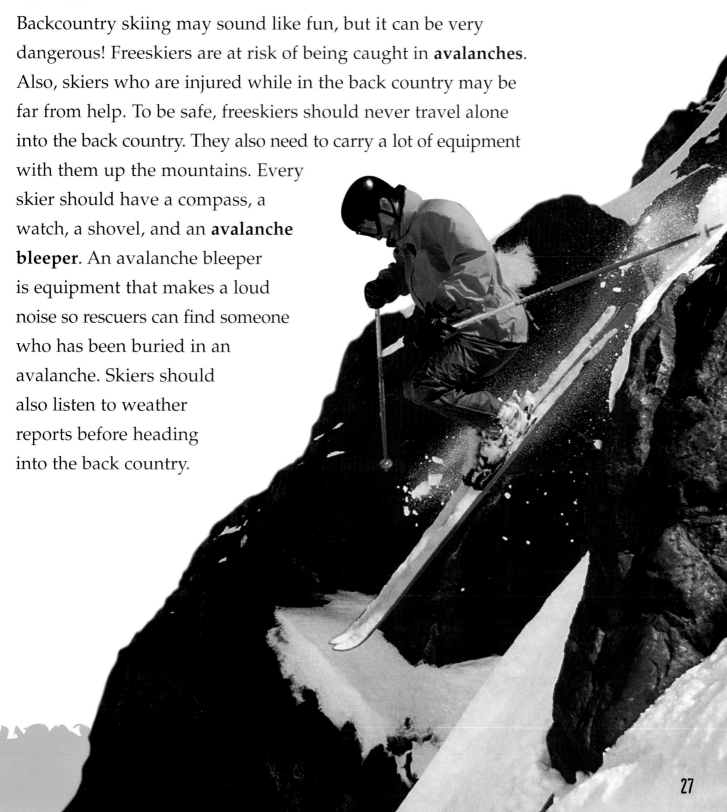

FAMOUS FREESTYLE SKIERS

Many talented freestyle skiers have put in years of training to bring their sport the recognition it deserves. Through tireless effort, these exceptional top freestyle skiers have encouraged one another to improve their sport through displays of courage, speed, and skill. These pages introduce a few of the skiers who have left their mark on freestyle skiing.

SARAH BURKE

Canadian skier Sarah Burke is considered by many to be the best freeride skier in the world. She has been dominating women's freeride competitions for years. She won four out of the five contests she entered in 2003, despite an injury to her left knee. Burke later won gold in the halfpipe event when it was added to the Winter X Games in 2005. She also took first place at the 2005 FIS World Championships.

JOHNNY MOSELEY

American skier Johnny Moseley, shown below, is one of freestyle skiing's best-known stars. After winning gold at the 1998 Winter Olympics in moguls, Moseley took home the silver medal for big air at the 1999 Winter X Games. Moseley is as famous for his tricks as he is for the medals he's won. At the 2002 Winter Olympics, he debuted the "Dinner Roll," the popular off-axis trick he invented.

Jennifer Heil

Canadian skier Jennifer Heil is one of the world's best mogul skiers! She won the gold medal in women's moguls at the 2006 Winter Olympics. In 2004, she claimed the World Cup overall women's mogul title and then went on to do it again in 2005! Heil also won the World Champion title in dual moguls at the 2005 FIS World Championships.

Eric Bergoust

American skier Eric Bergoust has been a fan of aerial skiing since he built a homemade jump at the age of thirteen. After years of training, Bergoust has come to dominate his sport. He has won thirteen World Cup titles, two U.S. Championships, and a gold medal in aerials in the 1998 Winter Olympics.

Kari Traa

Norwegian skier Kari Traa, shown below, has dominated women's mogul competitions with her incredible speed and creativity. After claiming the bronze medal for women's moguls at the 1998 Winter Olympics, Traa went on to win gold at the 2002 Winter Olympic Games, and silver at the 2006 Winter Olympic Games.

Freestyle skiing is an adventurous, creative way for people of all ages to stay fit and have fun. Before you try the fast-paced moves of the pros, however, you must first master the basics of skiing. Be sure to wear the proper safety equipment every time you ski. Always wear a helmet! You may also want to wear pads on your knees and elbows to help protect yourself from injuries.

Share the Slopes

A day on the slopes is much more fun when all the athletes respect one another. Remember that other skiers and snowboarders are also speeding down the slopes. Stopping suddenly on a hill or cutting off other athletes puts you and other people at risk. Skiers and snowboarders must also wait their turn in terrain parks and share the available equipment.

Beginners should keep in mind that top freestyle skiers train for years before successfully performing tricks.

TRAINED INSTRUCTORS

One of the best ways to increase your skills quickly is to take lessons from a trained freestyle skiing coach. A coach can teach you important safety techniques that will help you feel confident and in control on your skis. A coach can also help you decide which kinds of skis and equipment are right for you.

Once you feel confident on your skis, your skills will improve quickly and you can try new tricks!

GLOSSARY

Note: Boldfaced words that are defined in the text may not appear in the glossary

acrobatics Tricks that require great skill, balance, and flexibility

avalanche A wall of snow and ice that falls suddenly down a mountain

back country An area with few inhabitants

collide To run into something

double flip A trick that requires a skier to flip head-over-heels in midair twice before he or she lands

fiberglass A material made from glass fibers

flexible Able to bend easily without breaking

flip A trick that requires a skier to turn head-over-heels in midair

graphics Colorful images on the top skins of skis

immigrant A person who settles permanently in a new country

slopestyle An event in which skiers compete on a course filled with different types of obstacles

snow blindness A temporary loss of vision caused by exposure to very bright sunlight reflected off snow or ice

spin A trick in which a rider rotates in the air before landing

sponsor To pay an athlete to use a company's equipment or to wear its clothing

superpipe An event that takes place in a U-shaped ditch that has walls up to 18 feet (5.5 m) high

terrain An area of land with certain surface features, such as rocky mountains

terrain park An area filled with obstacles that are used for performing tricks

thermal Describes clothing that is designed to keep in body heat

ultraviolet rays Invisible waves of light that can cause cancer

upright A trick in which a skier's feet do not go over the skier's head while the trick is performed

X Games An annual series of extreme sports competitions

INDEX

1 2 3 4 5 6 7 8 9 0   Printed in the U.S.A. 5 4 3 2 1 0 9 8 7 6